A Small Book of
FAIRIES

Text by Eugene Stiles

POMEGRANATE ARTBOOKS *San Francisco*

Published by Pomegranate Artbooks
Box 6099, Rohnert Park, California 94927

Library of Congress Cataloging-in-Publication Data

Stiles, Eugene.
      A small book of fairies / text by Eugene Stiles.—1st. ed.
             p.   cm.
      ISBN 0-87654-476-6
        1. Painting, British. 2. Painting—18th century—Great Britain. 3. Painting—19th century—Great Britain.
      4. Fairies in art. 5. Fairies.
      I. Title.
      ND466.279   1995
      751'.7'094109033—dc20
                                    95-24184
                                    CIP

Pomegranate Catalog No. A804

Designed by Bonnie Smetts Design

Printed in Korea
00 99 98 97   6 5 4 3

First Edition

JOHN GEORGE NAISH, detail from *The Midsummer Fairies*

Fairies. *The very word conjures up visions of enchantment and magic, of the graceful, tiny winged figures who soared through the stories and dreams of our childhood. It summons to our imaginations a world of pageantry and mystery, of cheerful, fey creatures, charming and gay, who come in through the keyhole and disappear in the twinkling of an eye.*

SIR JOSEPH NOEL-PATON,
detail from *The Quarrel of Oberon and Titania*

Fairies possess enormous appeal. They are found worldwide, from the naiads and nymphs of ancient Greece to the jinns and genies of the Arab world and the peri of the Persians. They are found in Asia, in Africa, on the Pacific Islands, and among various tribes of Native American Indians. Among the numerous sorts of fairies are dwarves and elves, leprechauns and pucks, banshees and brownies. There are knockers (who inhabit the mines in Devon and Cornwall), spriggans (grotesque, malevolent beings from western England), Welsh seal fairies, and Scottish Kelpies (water spirits). There are goblins and hobgoblins, mermaids, mermen, dryads, undines, nixies and pixies.

JOHN ANSTER FITZGERALD, detail from *The Captive Robin*

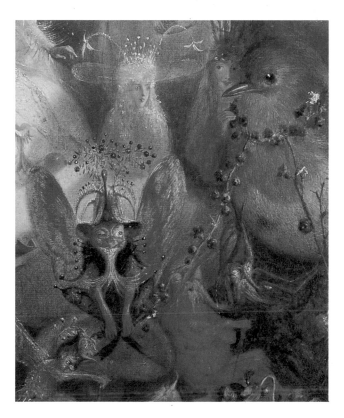

The "little folk." The "good neighbors." The "honest folk." The "gentry." These are some of the names that fairies were given, for they do not like to be called "fairies." The Irish call them the *sidhe*, pronounced *shee*, meaning "people of the hills," after the hills and mounds where they live. Other names are the "forgetful folk," the "people of peace," or the "mother's blessing." In many of these names we find the wishful thought that if these mischievous folk are named nicely, perhaps, just perhaps, they will then behave nicely.

Like the words *famous, fable, ineffable,* and *infant, fairy* ultimately goes back to an Indo-European root meaning "to speak." The original Latin root is *fata,* the name for the Fates, personified by

EDWARD ROBERT HUGHES (ENGLISH, 1851–1914)
Midsummer Eve

Private Collection
Photograph courtesy Fine Art Photographic Library Ltd., London

three women who spin and weave the destiny of each person's life. It traveled through the Latin *fatare*, meaning "to enchant," which in France became *faerie*, meaning "illusion, enchantment, magic." (The French word for an individual fairy is fée.) The word *fairy* can refer to illusion or enchantment, to a land of enchantment, to the beings who live in that land, or to specific individuals of this group of beings.

Most of us know about the "little folk" primarily from the fairy tales of our youth. In these stories there are generally two kinds of fairies: the evil ones (such as Rumpelstiltskin [Tom-Tit-Tot, in England], who wished to take a woman's first child in return for spinning an impossible amount of thread in a short time) and the benevolent ones, such as fairy godmothers. These good fairies appear and aid worthy people such as Cinderella, dressed up in finery to attend the king's ball.

Both benign and malevolent fairies always possess certain powers of magic or conjuring.

We also find fairy lore in works of literature and art as early as Chaucer's "Tale of the Wife of Bath" and the medieval romances. It remained popular with poets Edmund Spenser, Ben Jonson, John Milton, and W. B. Yeats. In the early accounts of fairies, including the romances of the thirteenth and fourteenth centuries, fairies are portrayed as human beings who possess superhuman powers of magic and enchantment. The fairies found in the Arthurian myths, such as Morgan Le Fey, may represent remnants of an older, goddess-worshipping culture driven underground by Christian invaders. By the time of Edmund Spenser's *The Faerie Queene* (1590–1596), fairies were portrayed as the diminutive elflike race we identify as fairies today.

William Shakespeare's *A Midsummer Night's Dream* is perhaps the best known of the literary and dramatic representations of the "little people." This play was a special inspiration to many of the fairy painters of Victorian England. Like all fairies, Shakespeare's are found in beautiful natural surroundings. Small in stature, graceful and comely, they value cleanliness and are quite mischievous. They love nighttime dancing and revelry. The social organization, headed by Titania, the queen, and Oberon, the King, echoes that of a medieval court. Although the fairies speak somewhat contemptuously of humans, they do like to meddle in human affairs. Titania and Oberon amorously pursue humans. Human infants, such as Titania's Indian boy, are brought to their land

FLORENCE VERNON, detail from *The Fairy Haunt*

Arrival of the King and Queen of Fairyland

Early twentieth-century book illustration
Private collection
Photograph courtesy The Bridgeman Art Library, London

to raise. Their use of magic includes an ability to insure that human offspring are born, and remain, healthy. Except for the occasional jest, they are benevolent to mortals.

The jester to the king is Puck, named for the type of spirit called "puck" (*pooka* in Ireland, *pwca* in Wales), who wanders throughout England delighting in playing devious pranks. When we first meet Puck, "that merry wanderer of the night," that "shrewd and knavish sprite" also called Robin Goodfellow, we find that he delights in frightening the maidens of the village, skimming milk, keeping beer from fermenting, and leading night-wanderers astray. He boasts how he will transform himself into a three-foot stool and then, when a housewife sits on him, topple her over. When he desires, he does work for humans and guarantees them good luck.

Our other sources of fairy lore are the history and traditions of the countryside of the British Islands, ranging from medieval chronicles to oral accounts collected in the last two or three centuries. Many of these tales are related by simple country folk whose stories of encountering fairies have a compelling and truthful quality, such as the account of two greenish tinged children found in a cave near Suffolk in the twelfth century. In these "real" encounters we see the basis for the portrayals in literature, tale, and art, although it may well be the interaction between all genres that creates the fairy folk as we know them.

The descriptions on record agree that fairies are a shy folk, somewhat difficult to see, who appear and disappear at will. In many of the portrayals they could well be a smaller-statured people who retreated to the woods to live, and this is, indeed,

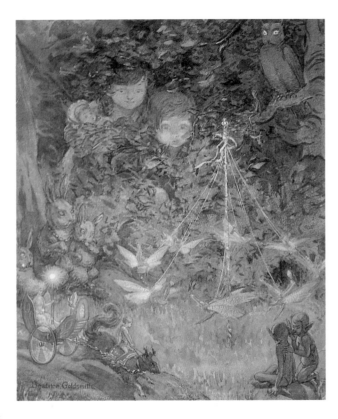

one theory about the origin of fairies. Generally, however, oral history portrays a group of beings whose magical powers definitely make them nonhuman.

Fairies are enchanting, in all senses of the word. People find them delightful and charming. They are able to place an illusion over things to make them appear other than they are; some claim that all their beauty and splendor are accomplished by a sort of mesmerizing magic called "glamour." They work many magics, such as extracting an essence from a food while leaving an empty husk behind, or creating something, such as a piece of cheese, that won't be diminished by use. They possess the power to cure or to harm. Like the

BEATRICE GOLDSMITH (1895–1947)
Watching the Fairies, 1925

© Chris Beetles Ltd., London
Photograph courtesy The Bridgeman Art Library, London

ARTHUR JOHN BLACK, detail from *Fairies' Whirl*

Fates, fairies have the gift of foresight and foreknowledge and can influence a person's luck to
good or ill. They fly through the air, often using a
stem of grass, hemp, or ragwort as transport.

There is something both charming and frightening about the "little folk." Anne Jeffries, an Eng-
lishwoman investigated as a witch in 1646, said
the fairies gave her healing powers. Other stories
tell of gifts of foreknowledge or good luck given
in return for a good deed done the "people of
peace." But often gifts appear to be at the whimsy
of the giver: of the many tales of human midwives
called to aid in fairy births, some were rewarded
with luck or money while others received only
thanks, and some barely escaped with their lives.

CHARLES ALTAMONT DOYLE,
detail from *The Fairy Queen—A Procession*

(Fairies also called upon human nurses to provide milk for fairy babies.) And for every story of a human spirited away by fairies, there is one of a mortal choosing freely to become a fairy's mate, such as that of the thirteenth-century poet Thomas of Ercildoune ("Thomas the Rhymer").

Fairies such as brownies (or pucks, boggarts, and pixies) are actually helpful, attaching themselves to a house or family and helping with chores such as cleaning or milking cows in return for a bit of milk and bread left on the hearth (a basin of water for pixies). Nonetheless, like all fairies, they love pranks, such as soiling clothes on the line, blowing out candles, or knocking on doors and walls. And should a human forget to give them their

FREDERICK MCCUBBIN,
detail from *What the Little Girl Saw in the Bush*

JOHN ANSTER FITZGERALD, detail from *The Fairy's Barque*

dinner or leave the place too much of a mess (for they value cleanliness), they can make life a misery by keeping the bread from rising or the ale from having a head, throwing things around, or even killing livestock. Despising idleness, they are apt to pinch lazy servants.

Perhaps the most appealing aspect of fairies is their merry nature and their revelry, their love of dancing and music. There are stories everywhere of people who, following enchanting and lovely nighttime music—be it harp, flute, or fiddle—come across a group of the "little folk" dancing at grass fairy rings. There is, however, a danger here: humans who join the dance can become bemused and lose track of time, dancing for days while thinking only minutes have passed.

It could be that the worst example of harm done by fairies is the stealing of human infants and leaving changelings, clever copies of the original human children, in their place. Adults are stolen, as well, such as one Grace Hutchins of West Cornwall, taken away to be a servant. A whole raft of ills was thought to be caused by fairies, including anything that twists or deforms the body, paralysis, bruises, and consumption. A man was lamed in the right leg because he inadvertently rode through a fairy market. Nearly any defect in an infant was blamed on a fairy, and a grossly deformed or retarded infant was said to be a changeling. Some wholly malevolent fairies lead travelers astray to their death. But fairies apparently have a morality that allows them to feel no remorse for their hurtful actions. In dealing with fairies, one must be very careful not to offend.

Fairies are great bargainers and expect bargains to be kept. Townspeople in Surrey could go to a certain cave, covered by a rock, and borrow

whatever they needed, as long as it was returned when promised. When a cauldron was not returned on time, the rock closed forever. (This cauldron was kept for many years in the church at Frensham in Surrey.) Likewise, whenever a man brought a fairy bride home, there was always some condition he had to fulfill. Wild Edric of Shropshire married a fairy woman, but she left when he forgot he was not to reproach her for her absences or question her about her family.

Fairies usually appear in human form, although up close some kind of defect may be detected, such as only four fingers, or nostrils without a nose. Usually smaller than humans, they range in size from one or two inches up to several feet,

ELEANOR VERE BOYLE, detail from illustration to *Thumbkinetta*

often changing their size at will. Many fairies are shapeshifters: a favorite trick for a fairy was to turn himself into a horse and entice an unsuspecting traveler to mount, only to toss the poor fellow in a stream. Solitary fairies may be old and wrikled or young and beautiful, whereas communal fairies are more often young and attractive. Many sightings of fairies on record do not include wings in their descriptions; even the twentieth-century clairvoyant Geoffrey Hodson reported seeing only some fairies with oval wings.

Fairies are seen both naked and clothed in all styles and colors of clothing. They are often dressed in the clothing of the districts where seen, usually in a more old-fashioned and elegant

ELEANOR VERE BOYLE, detail from illustration to *Thumbkinetta*

JOHN ANSTER FITZGERALD, detail from *The Captive Robin*

The Feast

Early twentieth-century book illustration
Private collection
Photograph courtesy The Bridgeman Art Library, London

manner. Green, brown, and gray are especially popular; the men often sport a cap or hat. Communal fairies are usually quite glamorous, sometimes attired in silky, flowing fabric. Specific types of fairies have their own characteristic attire. Thus the brownie, a homely and mostly good-natured spirit, appears as a small, shaggy man about two feet high, either naked or shabbily dressed in brown. The Irish Banshee, the pale woman spirit whose keening portends a death, has long teeth, eyes red from weeping, and is dressed in white.

Fairy cities are wondrous places found beneath hills or ancient burial mounds, under water, deep in the woods, or in a cavern. They may be in a land far away, often an island, such as the Isles of

ELEANOR FORTESCUE-BRICKDALE,
detail from *The Introduction*

21

the Blessed or Avalon, also called the Fortunate Isles. Visitors report great beauty and splendor, bejeweled towers of gold, and lovely flowers growing everywhere during all seasons of the year. Little people, dressed in great finery, play alluring music and dance. They enjoy many of the same activities as humans, such as riding horses, hunting, games, crafts (especially spinning and weaving), and sowing and reaping crops. These are lands of plenty and gaiety, free from death, disease, and unhappiness. In the words of Yeats:

> *The land of Faery, where nobody gets old and godly and grave,*
> *Where nobody gets old and crafty and wise,*
> *Where nobody gets old and bitter of tongue.*

ETHELINE E. DELL, details from *Fairies and a Field Mouse*

It is no wonder fairy lands had such names as the "Land of the Ever-Living," the "Land of Light," and the "Place of Happiness." Mortals easily lose all sense of time in these beguiling lands. When Bran, son of Febal, returned from Emhain, the Island of Women, after what he thought was one year of time, a thousand years had passed in the outer world, and his voyage had become the subject of ancient legends.

The picture that emerges of fairies, then, is of charming creatures of magic, who must be approached carefully lest they take offense. Whether real or imaginary, they have been found in hill and home, literature, story, and art for hundreds of years. In fact, most paintings of fairies date from the last two hundred years; an entire genre of fairy painting emerged during Victorian times. The nineteenth century was an era of rapid change and industrialization, which caused a somewhat uneasy feeling about science and the future. There was great interest in the unseen world. The fairy folk, with their closeness to nature and complete lack of modernity, must have offered a welcome diversion from the uncertainty of the rapidly changing world. The visual images of the "honest folk" from Victorian times remain familiar to us, for our conception of fairies essentially has changed little from the time of Shakespeare. The survival of fairies in the Age of Reason and the Victorian age is echoed by the survival of fairies in the human imagination even today.

RICHARD DOYLE, detail from *The Enchanted Tree*

SIR JOSEPH NOEL-PATON (BRITISH, 1821–1901)
The Quarrel of Oberon and Titania, 1849

Oil, 39 x 60 in.
© National Galleries of Scotland, Edinburgh

IDA RINTOUL OUTHWAITE (1888–1960)
Fairies Dancing

Pen and ink and watercolor
Chris Beetles Ltd., London, © LWM 1995
Photograph courtesy The Bridgeman Art Library, London

Mischievous and clever, fairies find their greatest pleasure in music and dance. On fairy mounds, in woods, and near streams they play their gentle, cheerful music and whirl and twirl all night under the moonlit sky.

John George Naish (1824–1905)
The Midsummer Fairies, c. 1856

Oil, 14 x 18 in.
© Christopher Wood Gallery, London
Photograph courtesy The Bridgeman Art Library, London

Have you heard of the land of fairy? A glorious place

under a greensward hill, lit with velveteen orbs of light,

a land of mystery and delight, all crystal and gold and

flowers and feathers with a great, gay laughter ringing

through the air.

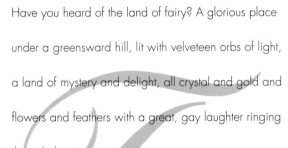

Joʜɴ Aɴsᴛᴇʀ Fɪᴛᴢɢᴇʀᴀʟᴅ, detail from *The Enchanted Forest*

CHARLES ALTAMONT DOYLE (1832–1893)
The Fairy Queen—A Procession, 1882

Watercolor
© The Maas Gallery, London
Photograph courtesy The Bridgeman Art Library, London

Detail from *The Feast*

ARTHUR RACKHAM, detail from *The Fairies in Spring*

Where the wave of moonlight glosses

The dim grey sands with light,

Far off by furthest Rosses

We foot it all the night,

Weaving olden dances,

Mingling hands and mingling glances

Till the moon has taken flight;

To and fro we leap

And chase the frothy bubbles,

While the world is full of troubles

And is anxious in its sleep.

(W. B. Yeats, "The Stolen Child")

ARTHUR JOHN BLACK (ENGLISH, 1855–1936)
Fairies' Whirl, 1893 (detail above)
Photograph courtesy Fine Art Photographic Library Ltd., London

Detail from *Arrival of the King and Queen of Fairyland*

ELEANOR VERE BOYLE (1825–1916)
Illustration to *Thumbkinetta*, by Hans Christian Andersen, c. 1872

ARTHUR RACKHAM (ENGLISH, 1867–1939)
The Fairy's Tightrope, from *Peter Pan*

Private collection
Photograph courtesy The Bridgeman Art Library, London

Over hill, over dale,

    Through bush, through briar,

Over park, over pale,

    Through flood, through fire,

I do wander everywhere,

Swifter than the moon's sphere . . .

(William Shakespeare, *A Midsummer Night's Dream*, Act II, Scene 1)

John Anster Fitzgerald (British, 1832–1906)
The Enchanted Forest

Photograph courtesy Fine Art Photographic Library Ltd., London

Edward Robert Hughes, detail from *Midsummer Eve*

RICHARD DOYLE (1824–1883)
Triumphal March of the Elf King

© British Library, London
Photograph courtesy The Bridgeman Art Library, London

There are several theories as to the origin of fairies. Some say they are the remnants of a diminutive, prehistoric race that were driven into the hills by successive waves of invaders. Others say that they are followers of the ancient goddess religion, forced to hide by the intolerance of the newer religions. Others, such as clairvoyant Geoffrey Hodson, say that they are beings made of more etheric streams of energy, lacking a solid body. They are thought by some to be fallen angels, those not evil enough to be consigned to hell but certainly not worthy of heaven. Still others would claim that they are merely ghosts.

ARTHUR RACKHAM, detail from *The Fairy's Tightrope*

JOHN ANSTER FITZGERALD (1832–1906)
Cat Among the Fairies

Private collection
Photograph courtesy Sotheby's, London

In Ireland, Oisin fell in love with the beautiful fairy woman Niamh, and they rode away on her white horse to Tir Nan Og, the land of youth. There they lived for many years, until the desire came upon Oisin to see his homeland. Niamh begged him to stay, but he would not be forestalled and rode back to the mortal world on the same white horse.

Now Niamh had warned Oisin not to touch the earth, but he slipped while helping some men raise up a stone. As he touched the ground he changed into a withered old man, blind and spent, for while he had dallied in the land of youth, that land of pleasure and delight, three hundred years had passed. If he had stayed in Tir Nan Og, he would be alive today, and Niamh would have her mortal lover to comfort her all her days.

JOHN ANSTER FITZGERALD (BRITISH, 1832–1906)
In Fairyland

Photograph courtesy Christie's Images, London

CHARLES F. ROBINSON, detail from *The Magic of the Cobweb*

JOHN ANSTER FITZGERALD, detail from *The Fairy's Barque*

JOHN ANSTER FITZGERALD, detail from *In Fairyland*

JOHN ANSTER FITZGERALD (BRITISH 1832–1906)
The Fairy's Barque, c. 1860

Oil, 10¹/₄ x 12¹/₄ in.
Private collection
Photograph courtesy The Bridgeman Art Library, London

O then, I see Queen Mab hath been with you.

She is the fairies' midwife; and she comes,

In shape no bigger than an agate-stone

On the forefinger of an alderman,

Drawn with a team of little atomies,

Over men's noses as they lie asleep.

(William Shakespeare, *Romeo and Juliet*)

53

Ida Rintoul Outhwaite, detail from *Fairies Dancing*

Frederick Goodall, detail from *A Fairy Scene*

There was once a humpback named Lusmore who lived in the town of Knockgrafton. One day, idling near a fairy mound, his ear was caught by the sound of wonderful song, delightful to hear. At a pause in the music, he deftly added his own words and so delighted the little folk of the mound that they pulled him inside and fed him and then, quick as you like, removed the hump he had worn since birth.

Well as it happened, word got around, and soon another humpback named Jack Madden slipped out to the same spot and, impatient to be healed, rudely thrust into the circle. He had no musical ability and stuck a most unmelodious phrase into the song. He was set upon and boxed soundly until he was unconscious, and when he awoke, the fairies had added the hump of Lusmore to his own.

JOHN ANSTER FITZGERALD (BRITISH, 1832–1906)
The Concert

Photograph courtesy Peter Nahum Ltd., London

RICHARD DOYLE, details from *Triumphal March of the Elf King*

It was a fairy place, all covered in magic and mystery.

Moving through the woods she fancied she could see

little folk flitting in and out amongst the trees. When

she broke into the clearing, there seemed to be glimpses

of wings resting on the noonday air. She waited

and waited, it seemed forever, and finally turned to

leave. Riding away she heard the tinkling of merry

laughter behind, but when she turned to look, all she

saw were the trees.

FREDERICK MCCUBBIN (1855–?)
What the Little Girl Saw in the Bush, 1904

Private collection
Photograph courtesy The Bridgeman Art Library, London

John Anster Fitzgerald, detail from *Rabbit Among the Fairies*

ELEANOR VERE BOYLE, detail from illustration to *Thumbkinetta*

Sir Joseph Noel-Paton, detail from *The Quarrel of Oberon and Titania*

ETHELINE E. DELL (BRITISH, FL. 1855–1925)
Fairies and a Field Mouse

Photograph courtesy Christie's Images, London

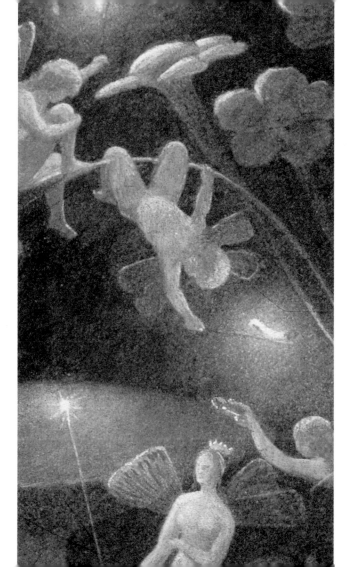

65

RICHARD DADD (ENGLISH, 1819–1887)
The Fairy Feller's Master Stroke, c. 1855–1864

Oil, 21 ¼ x 15 ½ in.
© Tate Gallery, London
Photograph courtesy The Bridgeman Art Library, London

We who are old, old and gay,

O so old!

Thousands of years, thousands of years,

If all were told . . .

(W. B. Yeats, "A Faery Song")

JOHN ANSTER FITZGERALD, detail from *The Concert*

John Anster Fitzgerald, detail from *In Fairyland*

ELEANOR FORTESCUE-BRICKDALE (1871–1945)
The Introduction
The International Fine Art Auctioneers
Photograph courtesy The Bridgeman Art Library, London

There was once an Irishman named Tom who caught a leprechaun, the little shoemaking fairy of Ireland. As much as the wee fellow screamed and hollered and begged to be put down, Tom refused to let the little man go until he promised to reveal the location of his buried treasure. And try as he might, the leprechaun couldn't trick Tom into looking away, for then the little fellow would have disappeared in the twinkling of an eye.

So, he was forced to lead Tom to his treasure, and before long they came to a ragwort plant where the gold was hidden. Tom thanked him kindly, let him go, and tied his red garter around the plant to mark the location while he ran off to fetch a shovel. Well, much to his dismay upon his return, wasn't just every ragwort bush for acres around tied with an identical red garter!

Richard Doyle, detail from *Triumphal March of the Elf King*

ARTHUR RACKHAM (ENGLISH, 1867–1939)
The Fairies in Spring, from *Peter Pan*

Private collection
Photograph courtesy The Bridgeman Art Library, London

I know a bank whereon the wild thyme blows,

Where ox lips and the nodding violet grows;

Quite over-canopied with lush woodbine,

With sweet musk roses, and with eglantine:

There sleeps Titania, sometime of the night,

Lulled in these flowers with dances and delight,

And there the snake throws her enamell'd skin,

Weed wide enough to wrap a fairy in.

(William Shakespeare, *A Midsummer Night's Dream*, Act II, Scene 1)

JOHN ANSTER FITZGERALD (BRITISH, 1832–1906)
The Sleeping Fairy

Watercolor, 5³⁄₈ x 5⁷⁄₈
Photograph courtesy Peter Nahum Ltd., London

Eleanor Fortescue-Brickdale,
detail from *The Introduction*

JOHN ANSTER FITZGERALD, detail from *Cat Among the Fairies*

CHARLES RENNIE MACKINTOSH, detail from *Fairies*

BEATRICE GOLDSMITH, detail from *Watching the Fairies*

WILLIAM H. SULLIVAN
The Fairy Ring

Oil on board, 5 x 3¾
Photograph courtesy Peter Nahum, Ltd., London

Come and dance!

Round and round

in joyous gambol,

Whirling and spinning

into the light of day!

JOHN ANSTER FITZGERALD (BRITISH, 1832–1906)
Rabbit Among the Fairies

Photograph courtesy Fine Art Photographic Library Ltd., London

CHARLES ALTAMONT DOYLE, detail from *The Fairy Queen—A Procession*

My cousin however saw a bright light and multitudes of little forms clad in crimson as well as hearing the music and then the far voices. . . . The queen of the troop came then—I could see her—and held a long conversation with us and finally wrote in the sand "be careful and do not seek to know too much about us."

(W. B. Yeats, *The Celtic Twilight*)

JOHN ANSTER FITZGERALD (BRITISH, 1832–1906)
The Captive Robin

Christie's, London
Photograph courtesy The Bridgeman Art Library, London

82

FLORENCE VERNON (BRITISH, FL. 1871–1905)
The Fairy Haunt

Photograph courtesy Christie's Images, London

Detail from *Arrival of the King and Queen of Fairyland*

JOHN GEORGE NAISH, detail from *The Midsummer Fairies*

Frederick McCubbin,
detail from *What the Little Girl Saw in the Bush*

By the moon we sport and play,

With the night begins our day;

As we dance the dew doth fall—

Trip it, little urchins all,

Lightly as the little bee,

Two by two, and three by three;

And about go we, about go we.

(John Lyly, "The Maydes Metamorphosis")

CHARLES F. ROBINSON (BRITISH, FL. 1874–1915)
The Magic of the Cobweb

Photograph courtesy Fine Art Photographic Library Ltd., London

Edward Robert Hughes, detail from *Midsummer Eve*

BEATRICE GOLDSMITH, detail from *Watching the Fairies*

89

It so befel, in that fair morning tide,

The fairies sported on the garden's side,

And in the midst their monarch and his bride.

So featly tripp'd the light-foot ladies round,

The knight so nimbly o'er the greensward bound,

That scarce they bent the flowers or touch'd the ground.

The dances ended, all the fairy train

For pinks and daisies search'd the flowery plain.

(Alexander Pope, *January and May*)

ELEANOR VERE BOYLE (1825–1916)
Illustration to *Thumbkinetta*,
by Hans Christian Anderson, c. 1872

© Victoria & Albert Museum, London
Photograph courtesy The Bridgeman Art Library, London

Richard Doyle (1824–1883)
The Enchanted Tree, 1845, a fantasy based on Shakespeare's *The Tempest*

Watercolor, 32 x 23 in.

Private collection

JOHN ANSTER FITZGERALD, detail from *The Sleeping Fairy*

Frederick Goodall (1822–1904)
A Fairy Scene

© Cecil Higgins Art Gallery, Bedford, England
Photograph courtesy The Bridgeman Art Library, London

IDA RINTOUL OUTHWAITE, detail from *Fairies Dancing*

Detail from *The Feast*